Copper Coast
A Coastal Community

Written by Maxine Keoghan
Illustrated by Jane Butler

Supported by

Comhshaol, Pobal agus Rialtas Áitiúil
Environment, Community and Local Government

ISBN 978-0-9572469-0-4

Benn

Tom

Victor

Take a trip along Copper Coast and meet the people who live and work there. Find out what Benn and Martha are up to. Where can Sophie be found? Is she with Tigerlily or having an ice-cream with Victor at Tom's? Come explore, there's so much more.

Sophie

Martha

Tigerlily

Annestown

Fenor Bog

Newtown Head

Boatstrand

Kilmurren

Ballydwane

Bunmahon Beach

Welcome to Copper Coast. Copper Coast is located in the south east of Ireland and begins at the adventure beach of Tramore and sweeps along to the west of County Waterford to the old pirate landing beach at Stradbally. From east to west the many beaches are well known by all in our community that care for them. The many beaches attract people wishing to swim, paddle or relax. The more adventurous can sail, surf or explore the caves in search of treasures washed ashore by the Atlantic Ocean.

During the summer when the school year has ended, families spend most sunny days at one of the many beaches of Copper Coast. Tramore has the longest beach and often people gather there to spend the day making sand castles and cooling down in the water. At one end of the beach when the tide goes out rock pools are formed which are quickly heated by the sun. Children love to splash about in the heated pools. Others take the opportunity to explore the seaweed covered rocks in search of crabs and tiny shrimp left behind by the retreating ocean.

Shrieks of excitement go out when a small boy nets a large crab whose pincers are nipping and whose eyes are bobbling.

Tramore bay is easily identified by the huge pillars at the mouth of the bay. At Newtown Head, three pillars stand tall. On the opposite side of Tramore Bay a further two pillars stand at Brownstown Head. The pillars were placed at Tramore Bay almost two hundred years ago as a warning system to keep ships from entering the bay and to prevent the bay from being mistaken for Waterford harbour. Today they stand as the maritime gateway of Tramore. A giant metal man stands on top of the middle pillar at Newtown Head. He looks far out to sea with his hand outstretched warning ships to stay away from Tramore Bay which is known locally as cemetery bay. It's called this because of the number of ships which entered the bay but never left. They now lie on the

bottom of the ocean. On calm nights it is said the ghosts return to claim their precious cargo they left behind.

~

The Coast Guard Station is located over-looking Tramore Bay and is the head quarters for the air, sea and cliff rescue crews that maintain a constant vigil of the ocean and the surrounding coastline. Martha Galvin is a member of the rescue squad and in the summer months Martha works as a life guard on Tramore beach ensuring people are safe. Martha often goes to the schools to explain to children the many dangers which can occur in the ocean and around the water edge. "All children should learn how to swim correctly by taking lessons", she explains. Most of the children of

Copper Coast learn to swim at a young age and enjoy surfing and other oceanic sports. The Tramore surf and adventure schools teach young people water safety. They also explain why the environment must be respected and indeed protected. Many visitors are attracted to Tramore to catch a wave or to hitch a ride on a blo-cart which can be seen zooming across the sands in summer and winter. Martha loves to surf and during her free time she is a member of the local surf team *The Wave Riders*.

Travelling from Tramore along the coast road we find the hidden beaches of Garrarus and Kilfarrasy. These beaches are always worth visiting as the jutting coastline seems to attract many different types of sea shells. A growing shell collector will be well rewarded with large razor shells and shiny black mussel shells found all along this isolated region. There are a number of bird species which also make this jagged coastline their home too. The kestrel is a small bird of prey and has a short, hooked bill for eating meat. The kestrel is easily identified as it hovers with a fanned tail when hunting for its prey. Another bird which makes Copper Coast its home is the chough who is a member of the crow family. Choughs are a most wonderful bird to study as their acrobatic antics are accompanied by sharp

"chaaow" calls. Choughs inhabit windswept coastal regions of Ireland such as Copper Coast giving rise to the name 'sea crow'.

One of the many folk lore stories of Copper Coast include the story of how choughs saved the entire region from a wealthy Baron. The Baron attempted to clear people from his lands and to prevent people from going to their beaches. The chough bravely fought the Baron who became exhausted  and weary of the small warriors and left Copper Coast and its inhabitants in peace.

The people of Copper Coast like to explore the natural environment to discover different plants and insects. The Copper Coast children go on nature trails in summer and autumn and display their collections at the Copper Coast Community Centre. Many of the community activities take place there. Benn Keoghan works at the Copper Coast Centre and oversees many of the projects undertaken by the community. Benn, like Martha is also a member of the Wave Riders Surf Club and loves to surf as often as he can. Today, Benn has decided to take the children to see some of the people who work and live in Copper Coast.

Benn takes the children on an eco-walk and first they visit the bog in Fenor. Benn explains to the children the importance of caring for the environment. People visit Copper Coast to see nature's beauty.
An eco-tourist is a visitor who likes to explore places in order to understand the ecology of the area. Ecology is the study of nature and the environment. It is also called the study of natural science. In the bog they walk along the boardwalk and find some

tadpoles in the marshy waters of the bog. Benn explains that it is not good to take the tadpoles from their home in the bog but he encourages the children to visit often to watch the tadpoles grow into frogs. In the summer the bog is alive with the colours and sounds of nature. Insects are buzzing while the birds and flowers add wonderful summer colour to the bog. Foxes can be seen at the bog but only if you're very quiet as they are shy animals and are often afraid of people.

After visiting the bog the group travel to Annestown which is a small picturesque seaside village. A short distance up the hill from Annestown beach, the cottages are brightly painted and are beautifully decorated with flowers during the summer.

Annestown beach is wonderful for swimming, it is also a great beach to fish. Many budding fishing girls and boys fish here or at the river that runs into the sea at this point. What is often more exciting than Annestown beach is the road that turns towards Dunhill Castle away from the small village. Heading towards the castle surrounded by the

reeds, the unsuspecting walker can face many dangers. Luckily, Victor Costello who lives along this small road leaves many warning signs. Victor is a great story teller but is also a bit of a trickster and may even be responsible for the warning signs which tell of bears and alligators.

The signs offer great excitement! Although no exotic animals live in Copper Coast, the attraction of dark shadows in the surrounding hillsides keep young imaginations active.

Dunhill and Annestown are located in the picturesque valley called the Anne Valley. It is here that an integrated wetlands has been constructed which filters farmyard waste through landscaped vegetated ponds and finally delivers fresh water to the adjoining Annestown river. This patchwork quilt of leafy ponds is a sanctuary for frogs and lizards while purple-bluish dragonflies hover and dart across the landscape in late summer.

Dunhill Castle is located in an environmentally protected area and as such becomes the number one location for black berry picking in August and September. A climb to the castle is easily done by following the meandering path, but the castle itself is not safe to explore as it is very old and could be damaged. Only the very brave will dare to find the old graveyard and church that once accompanied the castle in forming a settlement inhabited hundreds of years ago.

~

Close by Dunhill Castle, Benn introduces the children to Sophie Wheatley who is the Environmental Officer of Copper Coast. Sophie ensures that the water remains unpolluted by taking samples which are tested in the laboratory. Sophie encourages the children to help her. Large nets are given to the volunteers and water is kicked into the nets. The types of insects and the quality of the plants in the nets are noted by Sophie. The children are reminded that everyone should keep the river water clean and unpolluted.

Benn and the children continue along the beaches looking for others who work and live in our community. Over-looking Kilmurren Cove, they find the local artist Tigerlily Swift. Tigerlily loves to paint pictures of the coastline and its surroundings, she encourages the children to take part and gives them some drawing paper and pencils. Tigerlily tells the children of the different types of stone and rock which can be found along the cliffs of Copper Coast. Tigerlily loves to study the geographical nature of the landscape and also volunteers at the community centre with Benn where she teaches children how to paint and make crafts.

Tigerlily explains to the children that she will show them her collection of rocks and drawings inspired by the coastline when she returns to the community centre. After lunch Benn and Tigerlily take the children to visit the Tankardstown engine houses. Mining took place along Copper Coast many years ago. This is where the name Copper Coast came from as the miners were extracting copper from the area. Mining no longer takes place in Copper Coast but the small row of houses where

the miners lived can be seen in the next village of Bunmahon.

The terraced row of houses is very small and it has been many years since they have been lived in.

~

Tom Power is the local shopkeeper of Copper Coast, his shop is located in Bunmahon. *Copper Coast Stores* provides buckets and shovels, teas and coffees and many other surprises. The children love to visit his shop especially on sunny days. Tom offers a taste of ice-cream he has just made, 'fossil delight', Tom explains, named after the coral fossils which are found in the lime-stone on the beaches of Boatstrand and Dunabrattin.

Tom has a collection of fossils on display at Copper Coast Stores.

Other beaches to visit at Copper Coast include Ballydwane and Ballyvooney. The children laugh as Benn explains that gold can be found in the cliffs on the beach of Ballydwane but before the children go

scrambling in search of gold Benn explains to them that the only gold to be found is called 'fool's gold' and should not be extracted from the rock. The children search and discover many stones and fossils.

~

The group make the last stop of the day at the village of Stradbally. Benn, Tigerlily and the children travel to the last beach on the western side of Copper Coast. This beach is found by walking through an enchanted oak forest. Local people call Stradbally beach 'pirates cove', as many famous pirates found Stradbally an ideal location to hide smuggled goods and to stock up on drinking water. The amazing caves and caverns are displayed when the ocean has retreated. On the beach the caves can be explored and the high

watermark is visible. The rocks that spend most of their time under water reveal the marine life that exists there. Many thousands of mussels grow on the rocks while the caverns look like huge cathedral structures reaching up to the skyline.

~

The children reluctantly head home after a long day exploring Copper Coast. They ask Benn can they come back again and where will they go next time. Benn laughs and explains to the

children that there's plenty of people to visit and lots of places to see at Copper Coast. As Copper Coast is a coastline community many people work in or near the ocean such as fishing men and women, lifeguards, cliff and mountain rescue crews, surf instructors and sea rescue teams. Benn promises to bring the children on future trips to visit others who live and work in Copper Coast.